UNSELFISH

KiDS

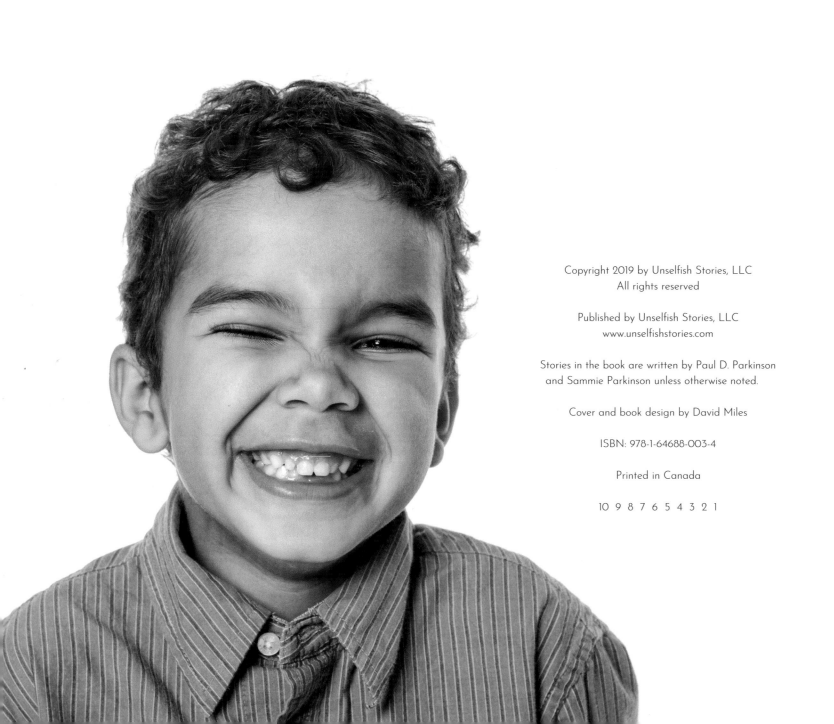

Published by Unselfish Stories, LLC
www.unselfishstories.com

Stories in the book are written by Paul D. Parkinson
and Sammie Parkinson unless otherwise noted.

Cover and book design by David Miles

ISBN: 978-1-64688-003-4

Printed in Canada

10 9 8 7 6 5 4 3 2 1

UNSELFISH Kids

PAUL D. PARKINSON AND
SAMMIE PARKINSON

CONTENTS

INTRODUCTION

FOUR YEARS AGO, WE WROTE AND PUBLISHED THE FIRST book in the Unselfish series titled *Unselfish: Love Thy Neighbor As Thy Selfie*. At the time, the term *selfie* had just been named the word of the year, and selfishness seemed to be at an all-time high. Four years later, selfishness appears to be holding strong.

We live in a world where we are exposed to a growing number of negative stories and divisive comments, even from those who are supposed to be examples to the younger generation.

But we don't believe that is how we were meant to live, and we especially don't believe that's how we need to live. **We believe that children can help change the course**—and *are* helping change the course! You'll read about just a few of them in *Unselfish Kids*.

As you read their stories, we invite you to make notes and write down your thoughts and ideas on page 94 at the end of the book. Have fun creating your own plan to make the world a better place; then, act upon that plan!

The unselfish acts we do don't have to be big to make a difference. In fact, most often it's the small things that create the big results.

Author Edward Everett Hale said: "I am only one, but I am one. I cannot do everything, but I can do something. And because I cannot do everything, I will not refuse to do the something that I can do."

Let's all do the something we can do!

A NOTE TO PARENTS, GRANDPARENTS, AND ALL THOSE WHO MENTOR CHILDREN

IT HAS BEEN SAID THAT CHILDREN MAKE UP ONE-third of our population but all of our future. What are we teaching our children to help them make the most of the future? How are we training them to make a difference in the world, no matter how small?

The last story in this book tells of fifteen-year-old Rhett Hering, who passed away too young. However, he left behind a legacy of kindness. As parents and grandparents, one of our greatest accomplishments can be raising children who are kind and who will one day also leave behind legacies of kindness and unselfishness.

Our children have endless possibilities. Spend time with any child, and it's as if you can hear them say, "Give me a little support, and I can do amazing things."

May we as adults support the children of the world and recognize the unlimited potential they have. Then, let's stand back and watch them do amazing things!

THE STORIES

HELP ME COLOR A RAINBOW!

SIX-YEAR-OLD ELLA TRYON WAS A PATIENT AT RAINBOW BABIES & Children's Hospital in Cleveland, Ohio. All she felt like doing was drawing and coloring rainbows with crayons. But her mom, Jackie, wasn't able to find good crayons for her to use. This made Ella think about other children in other hospitals who might also want crayons. So, after being released, Ella went to work.

As a first grader, Ella started a small campaign to collect crayons for children in hospitals. That summer, she set a big goal to collect 1,000 boxes of crayons by Christmas—but she collected that many in just three weeks! And after a few months, she had over 2,000 boxes! So, she courageously raised her goal to collect 10,000 boxes by October when she would have her next doctor's appointment at the hospital.

Today, just a few years after she started her first campaign, would you believe that Ella has collected more than 41,000 boxes of crayons for children's hospitals across the country? She has also set up a nonprofit organization called *HelpMeColorARainbow.com* where she is glad to accept donations. Her favorite part of her work is seeing the smiles on the children's faces when she delivers them crayons. "I just love making other people happy!" she says.

Ella's unselfish heart is seen in other ways, too. While visiting New York with her mom, she noticed a couple from Brazil with two young children. They had just received their US citizenship. Ella had been given a gift card for clothing, but when she saw this family, she said, "Mom, I think I need to give my gift card to them for their children."

In 2018, young Ella was named one of the 30 *Most Interesting People in Cleveland.* Her mom will tell you, "Kid's really can make a difference in the world." So far, don't you think Ella has made at least 41,000 differences?

THREE WISHES FOR RUBY'S RESIDENTS

IT ALL STARTED ONE DAY WHEN RUBY, WHO WAS ELEVEN, ASKED A FEW residents in a nursing home a simple question: "If I could bring you any three things in the whole wide world, what would they be?" Ruby's mom, who was a nurse for a local care center, was surprised by their answers. She said, "At first, Ruby thought they might ask for a new car or a big house, but instead, their wishes were very, very simple."

For example, one resident just wanted to have some fresh strawberries to eat. Another wanted a good book to read. Others wanted a phone because they felt lonely and didn't have anyone to talk to.

Ruby didn't know it, but there are over 1.5 million people living in nursing homes in America, and one million of them get only forty dollars a month from the government to pay for extra expenses like a haircut or a pizza night.

So, Ruby had an idea: she set up an account on GoFundMe.com to raise money, and her charity became known as Three Wishes for Ruby's Residents. So far, she has raised over $250,000! The first person she helped was a resident named Pearl. Pearl wanted to save her dog but couldn't with just forty dollars a month. Thanks to Ruby, now she could.

Ruby recruited Marilyn, a nursing home resident herself, to help find out what other people needed. Even though some people did need a little extra money, Ruby discovered that simply visiting with the residents could also help them feel less lonely.

Ruby says girls like different things and that some do dance or cheer or sports. She wasn't gifted in those areas, so she decided to make *kindness* her thing. Her mom says, "She's showing other kids less traditional ways to excel and be unselfish. And at the same time, she is shining a light on an often-forgotten population of beautiful souls in our care centers."

"IF I COULD BRING YOU ANY THREE THINGS IN THE
WHOLE WIDE WORLD, WHAT WOULD THEY BE?"

EVEN THOUGH
HIS WAS A
SIMPLE ACT—LIKE
MOST ACTS OF
KINDNESS—IT
MEANT A LOT
TO THE LADY HE
HELPED.

HE STOPPED TO HELP SOMEONE IN NEED

RUSH, RUSH, RUSH. DO WE EVER SEE SOMEONE IN NEED but say to ourselves, *I don't have time to stop and help right now, but I'll stop next time?* Gladly, this wasn't the case with eight-year-old Maurice Adams, Jr., of Georgia.

Maurice and his mom and sister were coming home from a high school graduation when they saw an elderly woman using a walker to slowly cross the road in front of them. Maurice had probably never heard the tale that if you help an old lady cross the road, you'll get a blessing in return. Well, once the woman had crossed, Maurice saw she was having a tough time getting up some stairs. So, he told his mom he needed to go help and jumped out of the car! He ran to the lady's side, put his hand on her back, and helped her up, one step at a time. When they had made it to the top of the stairs, he gave the lady a quick hug and went back to his mom's car.

Now, this story may not make the front page of the newspaper, but to that lady, that day, Maurice was an unselfish hero. And even though his was a simple act—like most acts of kindness—it meant a lot to the lady he helped.

LESSON #1: LOVE GOD.
LESSON #2: LOVE OTHERS.

By Billy Hallowell

"**A**CTIONS SPEAK LOUDER THAN *WORDS*." THIS IS SOMETHING MY SEVEN-year-old daughter, Ava, has been learning firsthand. You see, Ava has much more than many other kids her age. And sometimes, the more we have, the more blind we are to what others may need. That's why it has been important for me, as a dad, to teach my kids to not only appreciate what they have, but to notice what others may not have.

In our house, we're big on teaching two essential lessons: 1) to love God, and 2) to love others. So, we wanted to find a way to introduce Ava to practical ways she could love others. For instance, when Ava was five, we introduced her to an amazing website called Watsi.org. They allow people to crowdfund (fundraise) and use the money to help kids and adults who can't afford to pay for basic healthcare procedures.

Ava's eyes opened wide as she learned that with just a few extra dollars, we could make a life-changing difference: brain surgery, fixing broken bones, even eye procedures—there is no shortage of people who need help.

One day, Ava cracked open her wallet and offered to give her five-dollar allowance to help. That was really the beginning of her decision to love others by putting actions to her words. Now, nearly a year later, we still visit Watsi.org where Ava chooses which patients to help and follows their stories of hope and healing.

AVA'S EYES OPENED WIDE AS SHE LEARNED THAT WITH JUST A FEW EXTRA DOLLARS, WE COULD MAKE A LIFE-CHANGING DIFFERENCE.

2014

2015

2016

2017

BELLA SAYS SHE HAS ALL SHE
NEEDS AND WANTS OTHERS TO BE
BLESSED LIKE SHE HAS BEEN.

STILL BETTER TO GIVE
THAN TO RECEIVE

MY DAD'S BIRTHDAY FELL CLOSE TO CHRISTMAS, SO WE USUALLY JUST held back a Christmas gift or two to give him on his birthday. Since he was older and didn't really need that much, he didn't seem to care that he received only a few birthday presents. But Bella Broughton, whose birthday is also close to Christmas, asks her parents *not* to give her *any* birthday presents at all!

When Bella was four, she found out about some animals in an animal shelter near her home in Connecticut. She really felt bad for the animals, and so she told her parents that rather than give her birthday presents, she wanted them to use the money to buy supplies for the animals in the shelter. Then, for her fifth and sixth birthdays, Bella asked her parents to do the very same thing again. She felt a lot happier to be giving gifts to others instead of getting gifts for herself.

When Bella turned seven, this time she asked her parents to donate the money to help children who were in the hospital. Since Bella's birthday is just a few weeks before Christmas, she knew it would mean a lot for these children to receive a Christmas gift.

As Bella got older, she started to ask people outside her own family to help. She handed out flyers and posted requests for donations on social media. She even sent a letter to the president of a bank, who sent her a donation of $700! Because of this help from others, she was able to give much more to the animal shelter and to the hospital. Bella says she has all she needs and wants others to be blessed like she has been.

THE KINDNESS WARRIOR

WOULD YOU BELIEVE THAT ERIC PIBURN INVITED THE entire city of Tampa Bay, Florida, to celebrate his twelfth birthday party? His doctor had said that he probably wouldn't live to be even one year old, let alone twelve.

For the first twelve months of his life, Eric lived in the hospital more than he lived at home. During another year, he lived in the hospital for nearly seven months! You see, Eric needs a new heart and two new lungs, but because of the nature of his special immune disease, he's not eligible to receive these organ transplants.

In such a hard situation like this, Eric and his family had two options to choose from: to become bitter, or to become better. And which did they choose? You guessed it: Eric and his parents chose to become better. They couldn't control their situation, but they could control their reaction to it.

One important turning point happened when Eric started watching *The Ellen DeGeneres Show* and fell in love with the idea of being kind to one another. Eric would watch the show every day looking for examples of kindness, and that motivated him to start doing his own acts of kindness. He called himself "The Kindness Warrior" and went to work.

Since then, Eric and his family have shared many acts of kindness—big ones and small ones. They helped collect peanut butter to give to people who didn't have enough food. They volunteered for a group called Feeding Tampa Bay by helping hand out food to families in need. They gave out gift cards and flowers to random people with the help of a

"ERIC LOVES HELPING AND ENCOURAGING OTHER PEOPLE. EVEN THOUGH HE DOESN'T KNOW HOW LONG HIS TIME ON EARTH WILL BE, HE'S VERY DETERMINED TO MAKE A DIFFERENCE AS LONG AS HE IS HERE."

group called Hands Across the Bay. They even gave flowers to nurses, lunches to emergency responders, and presents to children in need.

His dad, Dave, says, "Eric loves helping and encouraging other people. Even though he doesn't know how long his time on earth will be, he's very determined to make a difference as long as he is here."

Eric says, "It makes me feel good doing acts of service to everyone. Besides, it's my job to make sure everyone gets exactly what they need. And it makes other people feel happy when we are kind."

"EVEN A SMALL
PERSON CAN MAKE
A BIG DIFFERENCE!"

CARTER'S CONCERTS FOR CHILDREN'S

By Kristen Davidson and Melisa Morrow

WHEN CARTER DAVIDSON WAS SEVEN, HE WAS WATCHING THE NEWS and saw a story about Children's Healthcare of Atlanta (they call it "Children's" for short). Right then, he asked his mom if he could help raise money for them. Carter had been taking guitar lessons since he was five, so he thought he could host a benefit concert. He didn't think of reasons why he *couldn't* do it—he just thought of reasons why he *could* (and should) do it!

It was nearly five years ago when Carter's mom first called to tell me about this concert Carter was planning. Fast forward a few years, and he has continued to hold a concert every year to raise money for Children's. He's twelve now, and the concert seems to get bigger each year. One recent concert included a special performance with John Driskell Hopkins of the Zac Brown Band. Carter invited radio celebrities and friends and families to the great event and entertained everyone by playing his own guitar and singing.

Last year, Carter was able to donate over $6,000 to the music therapy charity at Children's, and since he was seven, he has raised over $10,000. He was even selected to play a guitar piece called "Here Comes the Sun" by the Beatles in front of over one thousand people.

Carter seems to be wiser than his twelve years and is using his talent to benefit others' lives. As Carter has said many times, "Even a small person can make a big difference!"

USING HIS SAVINGS TO HELP HIS CLASSMATES

MOST NINE-YEAR-OLD KIDS KNOW IT'S HARD TO EARN MONEY—AND EVEN harder to save it. Ryan Kyote is like most nine-year-old kids; when he gets his allowance, he has a goal to save part of it. With his savings, he sometimes buys sports gear since he loves sports. When Ryan is saving, he's making a sacrifice: not buying something right now so you can save up longer and spend it on something you want even more.

By May of 2019, Ryan's school year was ending. He had heard the story of a five-year-old girl in another school who wasn't allowed to eat school lunch because she didn't have enough money. He asked his mom if there might be kids in his own school who also didn't have enough money to pay for school lunches. His mom found out that some kids in Ryan's third-grade class sometimes ate lunch but couldn't pay for it, and that their parents owed the school $74.80. The school district had a rule where they would always let students eat—even if they didn't have enough money—but that the parents still got a bill.

Ryan's mom, Kylie, asked Ryan what he wanted to do. He said he wanted to pay the entire $74.80 so his classmates would not owe anything by the time the school year ended. He wanted all his classmates to feel cared about and to be happy as they started their summer. Ryan used his allowance savings and paid the school for the whole bill—$74.80—but he didn't want any of his friends to know that he did it.

Even though he knew it would take extra time to save up again to buy sports gear, he learned that there are more important things in life than just buying stuff for ourselves—and those more important things usually involve friends.

RYAN USED HIS
ALLOWANCE SAVINGS AND
PAID THE SCHOOL FOR
THE WHOLE BILL—$74.50—
BUT HE DIDN'T WANT ANY
OF HIS FRIENDS TO KNOW
HE DID IT.

SHARE HOPE USA

WHEN SYMOND BOSCHETTO WAS EIGHT, HE HAPPENED TO SEE A homeless man just off the freeway exit on the way home from school. He asked his dad why some people like him didn't have a home. His dad explained the many reasons why it seems so many people are homeless and that it's sometimes complicated to understand the reasons. Symond was concerned about those people, and it seemed like a light just turned on in his mind.

Symond went right to work to try to help homeless people. His dad helped him start a nonprofit, ShareHopeUSA.com. In the four short years since that time, he and his group have helped to clothe, feed, and give haircuts to over 8,000 homeless people. They even groomed their pets!

Each month, Symond sets up a special outreach event where homeless people can come to get some help. Many other kind people join in by bringing food, clothing, hygiene items, pet food, and much, much more.

Symond understands better now that these people didn't want to be homeless and that, for whatever reason, they now find themselves in a really tough situation. He loves the saying, "Their reason for being homeless is irrelevant; their need for compassion isn't."

This wasn't the only good thing Symond wanted to help with. When he was still eight, he decided to collect Play-Doh to give to children's hospitals in the Los Angeles area. He held a Play-Doh drive every year, and four years later, he has collected and donated over 43,000 containers!

His dad, Russell, says, "Symond has a huge heart and loves everybody." Symond says, "The goals I want to accomplish are helping the homeless and getting as many donations as I can. I think I can make a difference. It makes me feel happy helping others."

"THEIR REASON FOR BEING HOMELESS IS IRRELEVANT; THEIR NEED FOR COMPASSION ISN'T."

NOAH'S ARK

By Leigh-Ann Haas

WHEN I WAS TWENTY WEEKS PREGNANT WITH OUR SON, NOAH, WE WERE TOLD HE had a hole in his heart that would need to be fixed soon after he was born. So, we talked to doctors at Children's National in Washington, DC, and made a plan. It didn't go as smoothly as we expected, and Noah couldn't have surgery until he gained more weight. He finally had heart surgery when he was only five weeks old. During the next eight months, he spent a lot of time in the hospital and had even more surgeries.

The caring and compassionate people at Children's National helped us get through our darkest times. We like to think that the charming personality Noah has developed was due in part to the amazing nurses who cared for him, alongside his father and me, day in and day out. In May of 2010, Noah was finally healthy enough to stay home with us.

In May of 2017, when Noah was seven, he was asked to help the First Lady of the United States, Melania Trump, with the ribbon cutting ceremony for the opening of the Healing Garden at Children's National. Noah happened to see a poster advertising the hospital's annual Race for Every Child, a 5K event that raises money for the hospital every October. Noah said, "I want to do that—I want to have a team!" That's when "Noah's Ark" was created. At the "race" event in October of 2018, his "Noah's Ark" team raised thousands of dollars to give to the hospital—the same hospital which gave him his life. Noah became a Race Ambassador and helped more people know about the Race for Every Child. He was also the official starter of the race.

For the past nine years, Noah and our family have also held a December toy drive. We donate the toys to children in the hospital so they can have a happier Christmas even though they are away from home. Noah loves seeing the smiles on the children's faces when they get these toys.

"I WANT TO DO THAT—I WANT TO HAVE A TEAM!"

BEAR SHARE

W HEN JULIANNA GOUTHIERE WAS six, her mom, Amanda, told her a story about when she was a young girl riding on the back of her dad's motorcycle. They got in an accident, and a fireman who came to help gave Amanda a teddy bear to comfort her. The bear really calmed her down.

After Julianna heard her mom's story, she wanted to do the same thing—give stuffed animals to children to help them feel better in difficult situations. So, Julianna began collecting stuffed animals. It has been five years now, and she has donated over 17,000 stuffed animals to children who were going through tough times!

Some of the stuffed animals were used by the Bossier Parish sheriff's office, who gives them to children when they are around a crime investigation. The Louisiana Foster Parent Association gives them to foster children. Shriner's Hospital for Children gives them to young patients in their hospital.

Julianna is just trying to do her small part to make the world a better place.

LIFE SAVINGS—SAVING LIVES

ONE SATURDAY AFTERNOON, RILEY LAFRENZ WAS WATCHING the University of Iowa Hawkeyes playing football on TV. The game was at Kinnick Stadium, which is right next to University of Iowa Stead Family Children's Hospital. At the end of the first quarter, the fans in the stadium stood up and started waving at hundreds of young patients and families who were looking out the big windows of the hospital.

Riley was nine, and he felt inspired by what the fans did to acknowledge those children in the hospital. He wanted to do something, too. He had been saving money to buy some NFL Football cards. But after seeing this on TV, he decided to take all his savings and donate it to the children's hospital—all $34.01! He sent his money to the hospital, along with a note he wrote:

> Hi! My name is Riley. The reason I sent the money is that when I watched a Hawkeye football game, I saw a kid that had cancer, and I felt sad, so now I realized that you need the money more than I do.
>
> From your friend,
>
> Riley
>
> Go Hawks!!

Riley said, "I hope it can get all the kids out of the hospital and maybe save some more sick kids that come in after that."

"I HOPE IT CAN GET ALL THE KIDS OUT OF THE HOSPITAL AND MAYBE SAVE SOME MORE SICK KIDS THAT COME IN AFTER THAT."

A lot of other people heard about Riley's donation, and it inspired them to donate to the hospital as well. Riley's mom, Missie Lafrenz, wrote on Facebook:

I hope this inspires others to "give more than they get" this Christmas season and all year 'round! It's amazing how infectious love and kindness can be.

"IT MAKES ME FEEL GOOD, BECAUSE I KNOW
THAT I'VE HELPED A LOT OF PEOPLE."

SNUGGLE SACKS: HOPE FOR THE HOMELESS

By Stacy Daul

ADDISYN GOSS WAS EIGHT WHEN SHE MET HER GRANDPA FOR THE FIRST TIME. SHE DIDN'T know he had been homeless for many years. Her grandpa told her and her siblings some stories about those hard times. Touched by his stories, Addisyn came up with a plan to help homeless people who lived in her town.

At first, Addisyn used social media to ask her family and friends to donate simple items such as toiletries, snacks, socks, gloves, and water. She got enough items to pack about fifty complete "survival" sacks and then went with her family to their local soup kitchen to hand them out. On this first delivery, they quickly learned these survival kits were sorely needed—nearly 200 people wanted one.

Addisyn wanted to keep going, so she joined up with her sister, Sheridan, and her brother, Jaxson, and SnuggleSacks.org was born. They now have their own warehouse where youth groups, companies, sports teams, and friends come to assemble the sacks and help with distribution. Each sack has about forty items to help people survive on the streets.

Since 2015, their team has donated over 10,000 sacks full of goodness to homeless people in Michigan. They partner with local shelters, churches, soup kitchens, and government agencies to hand out sacks to the people who need them most. They even have helpers in other states who run the Snuggle Sacks program in their own towns. Snuggle Sacks has been featured on the *Today* show, in the *New York Times* and *USA Today*, and in local news.

Addisyn is now eleven and serves on the Kids Board of Directors for Kidbox, a kids' fashion company in New York City. They donated clothing for her to give to kids in need in her community.

About her service, Addisyn says, "It makes me feel good, because I know that I've helped a lot of people." It gives them hope, she says. Her hope is that more kids will see that it doesn't matter how old you are—if you want to make a difference, with a little hard work, you can!

SMALL PUSH FOR A STRANGER

JUST BEFORE A COLD THANKSGIVING IN 2018, JOSH CUZDEY AND HIS MOM WERE pulling up to a grocery store near Albany, New York. Josh was looking out the car window and saw a man struggling to make it through the snowy parking lot in his wheelchair. He was holding grocery bags and having a hard time making much progress.

Josh, who's eleven, could see there was no one else helping the man, so he jumped out of the car and started pushing the wheelchair. While they talked, Josh learned that the man had lost his right leg, didn't have a car, and was trying to get back to where he lived at the Tompkins Motel—nearly a mile away.

When Josh's mom saw him pushing this stranger away from the grocery store, she started the car and drove towards them. She was surprised when Josh explained what was going on. He then asked his mom if they could give the man a ride home. She hesitated for a moment, but with Josh's persistence, they loaded the wheelchair and the grocery bags in their van, helped the man get in, and drove him back home.

Doing kind things like this isn't new to Josh. For instance, each year at Christmastime, he donates food to the hungry and even gives some of his own gifts to Toys for Tots. He has learned to serve all year round. This particular act of kindness in the snowy parking lot just happened to be a little more spontaneous than others.

For coming to the aid of a stranger, the Albany County Executive named Josh "Citizen of the Month" for November, 2018. When the honor was presented, the executive told everyone that Josh wasn't trying to get recognition by helping the man. Instead, "he did it because he saw a gentleman who was struggling to cross the street in his wheelchair." The man who Josh helped, whose name is Keith, was also present, and he said, "It gives me hope for the future that there are young people like Josh doing what he does."

"IT GIVES ME HOPE FOR THE FUTURE THAT THERE ARE
YOUNG PEOPLE LIKE JOSH DOING WHAT HE DOES."

TWO BOYS AND A LEMONADE STAND

By Heather Paglino

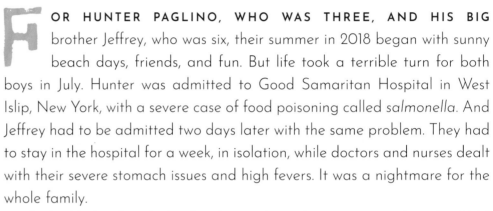

F OR HUNTER PAGLINO, WHO WAS THREE, AND HIS BIG brother Jeffrey, who was six, their summer in 2018 began with sunny beach days, friends, and fun. But life took a terrible turn for both boys in July. Hunter was admitted to Good Samaritan Hospital in West Islip, New York, with a severe case of food poisoning called *salmonella*. And Jeffrey had to be admitted two days later with the same problem. They had to stay in the hospital for a week, in isolation, while doctors and nurses dealt with their severe stomach issues and high fevers. It was a nightmare for the whole family.

The highlight of each day for the two boys, however, was when the Child Life team at the hospital came to visit. It brought needed smiles to the young boys as they enjoyed sing-alongs, made crafts, played video games, and did other fun things.

Thankfully, the boys recovered, and after a few more weeks they were able to resume their normal summer activities. But Jeffrey was so touched by the caring staff that had helped cheer him up while he was in the hospital that he told his mom about an idea he had to give something back. His idea was to host a lemonade stand and donate all the money they made to the Child Life Program at Good Samaritan Hospital.

So, the boys worked hard and made signs, stirred lemonade, and baked cookies for their special sale. Through the generosity of family, friends, and strangers, the boys raised $150 in just one day! The boys were so excited

HIS IDEA WAS TO HOST A LEMONADE STAND AND DONATE ALL THE MONEY THEY MADE TO THE CHILD LIFE PROGRAM AT GOOD SAMARITAN HOSPITAL.

All Money Will Be Donated To Good Samaritan Hospital Child Life Department

Lemonade
50¢

ookies
50¢

about their successful lemonade stand and were soon invited to visit the hospital to present their money to the Child Life team and staff who helped take care of them. Their donation will help other kids who have to go to the hospital enjoy some smiles and fun during their stay.

Hunter and Jeffrey learned some important life lessons as patients *in* the hospital and as unselfish donors *to* the hospital.

EACH OF US HAS BEEN GIVEN
DIFFERENT GIFTS AND TALENTS,
AND WE GET TO CHOOSE HOW
WE CAN USE THEM TO BLESS
THE LIVES OF OTHERS.

THE PIANO PLAYER

CHRISTOPHER NGUYEN BEGAN LEARNING HOW TO PLAY the piano when he was five, and it was easy to tell he had a natural talent for it. When he was seven, he started playing the piano for people who lived at a care center called the Waters Edge Lodge. Christopher is twelve now, and he's still volunteering to entertain the people who live at the Lodge, many of whom have become close friends. Playing the piano for these elderly residents makes him very happy.

"The seniors living at the Waters Edge Lodge look forward to Christopher coming on Fridays after dinner to play the piano, and new residents and visitors are amazed when they see his talent and can hardly believe he is able to play at such an incredible level," said Stephen Zimmerman, Chief Operating Office of AEC Living, who operates the Lodge.

Each of us has been given different gifts and talents, and we get to choose how we can use them to bless the lives of others. In Christopher Nguyen's case, he learned this important lesson early in his life, and he continues to find great happiness in sharing his gift with others.

PAUL DIDN'T THINK OF KAMDEN AS BEING DIFFERENT—HE JUST SAW HIM AS BEING A FRIEND.

I SEE HIM AS MY FRIEND

GOING TO KINDERGARTEN WAS NOT GOING TO be easy for Kamden Houshan. He was nervous and worried that other children might tease him because he always had to use a wheelchair to get around. So imagine how excited he was when he met Paul Burnett right when they entered kindergarten, because Paul didn't think of Kamden as being different—he just saw him as being a friend.

You see, ever since Kamden was a baby, he has had a large tumor inside his back near his spinal cord that makes it so he can't walk. He has had to use a wheelchair his whole life. As Kamden grew up, he began to outgrow his wheelchair, but his family's insurance would only pay for a new wheelchair once every five years. His family didn't have enough money to buy a bigger wheelchair.

Paul could see that Kamden was having a hard time with his small wheelchair. So, when school got out at the end of second grade, as a true friend, Paul decided he was going to do something about it. He had seen fundraisers on the Internet and knew he could do something to raise money. In two weeks, Paul was able to raise over $6,000—enough to buy Kamden a custom wheelchair that fit better!

And to think all of this started when a five-year-old boy decided to see a new classmate as a friend—not as someone who was different.

PEACE. LOVE. BRACELETS.

WHEN BELLA FRICKER WAS NINE, SHE HEARD about four kids in her community who had cancer. Having cancer can be a very difficult time for any child, and it seems to get worse when many of them lose their hair due to the medicines they have to take.

Bella wanted to do something to help these four kids, so she began making and selling bracelets. With the money she earned, she bought American Girl dolls that didn't have any hair and gave them to these four children. She kept making bracelets and was able to give dolls to many others. She now calls her small business "Peace. Love. Bracelets." She runs her business out of her playroom where she makes the bracelets and packages them up for shipping.

Some of the most memorable times for Bella are when she is able to meet some of the people who get her dolls. It makes her very happy seeing smiles on their faces and knowing she has done something to help someone who is going through a challenging time. So far, Bella has purchased thirty-eight new dolls to give to children in the hospital.

Bella knows something about health challenges herself. She has to deal with Type 1 diabetes, for which there is no known cure. But she doesn't let that slow her down. She is also working on creating care kits for children who have diabetes!

SO FAR, BELLA HAS PURCHASED THIRTY-EIGHT NEW DOLLS TO GIVE TO CHILDREN IN THE HOSPITAL.

LUCY'S STITCHED HUGS

By Holly Crouse

LUCY SAYS SHE SEWS A PIECE OF HER HEART INTO EVERYTHING SHE MAKES AND THAT SHE IS HAPPIEST WHEN SHE IS DOING SOMETHING FOR SOMEONE ELSE.

LUCY CROUSE IS A LITTLE GIRL WITH A BIG IDEA—AND AN EVEN bigger heart.

It all started when Lucy was nine. After seeing her mom and grandma making humanitarian quilts, she had an idea—a *big* idea—and wanted to make quilts for kids who could use a hug. That's when Lucy's Stitched Hugs was born. With help from her mom, Lucy made over thirty-six pies, which she sold to friends and family to earn money to buy sewing supplies. A few friends also donated some fabric.

Two years of stitching later, Lucy has donated over 200 quilts and 100 stuffed animals and pillows. Most have gone to a local organization that helps homeless families, and some have gone to refugee families. Along the way, she decided to sell her own Legos to earn money for supplies. And instead of getting birthday and Christmas gifts, you guessed it: she asks for more supplies! For her last birthday party, Lucy had a "Service Sew-cial" where she put friends and their moms to work stitching quilts.

Lucy and her big sister know firsthand how important it is to be kind to others as they both have autism. Lucy says she sews a piece of her heart into everything she makes and that she is happiest when she is doing something for someone else. She hopes her gifts of kindness make others feel loved. Because, after all, kindness and love are what make the world work.

LIAM'S LUNCHES OF LOVE

IAM HANNON JUST DIDN'T WANT TO GO TO SUMMER camp. However, his dad, Scott, wanted to make sure ten-year-old Liam stayed busy doing something positive during the summer. They found an online game called Brain Chase that challenged players to be productive, including giving service to their community.

Every week as part of the game, Liam would get a certain challenge to do service. The service challenge the first week was to help homeless people. So, his dad suggested they rent a food truck and hand out food. But Liam quickly pointed out, "There are people right outside our own apartment building. Why don't we just make them lunch?"

Liam and his dad made sandwiches in their apartment kitchen and packed them in brown sacks. Then they loaded up a wagon and walked the streets of Cambridge, Massachusetts, handing out the lunches. Liam was immediately hooked. His dad said, "That first week we made 20 lunches—that was going to be it. But then Liam asked, 'Dad, can we do this again? I like doing this!' So, we kept doing it, and each week it grew a little bit more." And that's how Liam's Lunches of Love started.

Since that small beginning, Liam has raised over $44,000 to help feed people who are homeless and has passed out thousands of bagged lunches. He adds kind notes and drawings to every bag. Liam's dad says, "The best part of this has been seeing Liam realize the effect *one person* doing something can have."

Liam says, "I've seen people who are feeling really down on themselves. But when we hand them a lunch, their faces just light up!"

"I'VE SEEN PEOPLE WHO ARE FEELING REALLY DOWN ON THEMSELVES. BUT WHEN WE HAND THEM A LUNCH, THEIR FACES JUST LIGHT UP!"

KHLOE KARES

ON HER WAY TO SCHOOL EACH MORNING, Khloe Thompson would pass by homeless people and wonder to herself why she was so lucky to have a home and why these people didn't. Even though the thought bothered her, she wondered if she could really do anything about it since she was only nine.

Khloe started to design and sew handbags with her grandma, Betty, and then filled the bags with important items like toothpaste, soap, toothbrushes, and shampoo. Khloe and her mom then delivered them to people who needed them. This was the beginning of her idea, which she called Khloe Kares.

One of the most memorable experiences for Khloe was at the LA Mission when a lady said to her, "You make me feel like a human being!" Khloe realized that there was a lot more to what she was doing than just handing out handbags of essential supplies. She was actually helping others realize their self-worth.

Young Khloe says about her mission: "I want to inspire other kids to be great and to make their mark on this earth. *It's time to make a difference!*"

"I WANT TO INSPIRE OTHER KIDS TO BE GREAT
AND TO MAKE THEIR MARK ON THIS EARTH.
IT'S TIME TO MAKE A DIFFERENCE!"

"I HAVE DECIDED MY LIFE WILL BE ABOUT GIVING—NOT TAKING."

MY LIFE WILL BE ABOUT GIVING

By Sheryl K. Lowry

ON GARRETT LOWRY'S SEVENTH BIRTHDAY, HE ASKED IF HE COULD donate his presents to kids who were less fortunate. There happens to be a Ronald McDonald House in Orange County, California, who helps families of children receiving medical attention, so Garrett delivered his presents to them. Then in 2012, Garrett asked for help to organize a team for Walk for Kids and raised hundreds of dollars in support of Ronald McDonald House.

When Garrett was in fifth grade, he wanted to be part of a project that was helping kids with cancer. With his grandmother's help, he began loom knitting caps and then donated them to Children's Hospital of Colorado in Denver. The caps help young patients feel more comfortable while they have to be in the hospital. So far, Garrett and his grandmother have knitted over fifty caps!

Garrett knew some people who had endured cancer, including family members and pets. But he became more aware of childhood cancer after meeting a young girl by the name of Riley Rose Sherman. She had a cancer of the nervous system called neuroblastoma. Garrett followed Riley's battle and saw how hard it was for her parents both emotionally and financially. Sadly, Riley Rose lost her battle with cancer in April, 2018.

All these experiences motivated Garret to start a philanthropic foundation in Riley's memory, which he called The Golden Rose Cancer Foundation. He hopes this will financially help families who are fighting pediatric cancer and fund more pediatric cancer research.

"Life is about taking the risks," Garrett says. "I want to live my life by putting everything on the line for others. I want to help kids that aren't as fortunate as I was growing up. I have decided my life will be about giving—not taking."

SANDRO'S COAT RACK

ANDRO CUNNINGHAM AND HIS MOM WERE watching TV one day and saw a news story about people in their town who didn't have a place to live and needed help. Sandro asked his parents how he could help. They thought it would be a great idea to provide warm coats for people who didn't have one since they live in New Jersey where it gets very cold in the winter.

Sandro, who is seven, began asking for donations of coats through his Facebook page, and people also left coats at special drop boxes in his town. He collected over 1,000 coats! He and his dad then built a rack on which to hang the coats, which they called Sandro's Coat Rack, and set it up close to the Trenton Area Soup Kitchen. They later moved the coat rack to be close to the police station where his dad works. Sandro put this sign on the rack:

Are you cold? Take one.
Do you want to help? Leave one.

Burlington Stores recently donated 1,000 new coats to Sandro's Coat Rack and a check for $5,000 for the Trenton Area Soup Kitchen. Sandro says, "I feel very excited, very, very good inside. I never knew this would help 1,000 people!"

RATHER THAN THINK ABOUT HER OWN PROBLEMS, SHE THOUGHT ABOUT OTHER CHILDREN AROUND HER IN THE HOSPITAL WHO MIGHT BE FEELING SCARED.

ALEX'S FLUFFY BUDDIES

WHEN ALEX WALKER WAS ELEVEN months old, she was diagnosed with epilepsy. It caused her body to have seizures, and she had to spend a lot of time in the hospital while she was growing up. But rather than think about her own problems, she thought about other children around her in the hospital who might be feeling scared.

Luckily, Alex had Sky Bear, a teddy bear that comforted her during all her treatments in the hospital. But Alex saw that many children didn't have a stuffed animal, and she felt sorry for them. She decided she would help get them their own stuffed animals to have with them in the hospital and came up with the idea of Alex's Fluffy Buddies. Since then, she has donated over 1,500 Fluffy Buddies to children in hospitals! Alex likes to deliver them personally, using her wagon to pull them up and down the hallways.

Alex's Fluffy Buddies donates to the Ronald McDonald House, local hospitals, women's shelters, foster care programs, and police and fire departments. And when she learns of someone living out of state who needs a special friend, Alex even mails the bears!

BELLA'S BIRTHDAY BOXES

ELLA SMITH IS IN THE THIRD GRADE, AND SHE WAS SURPRISED TO learn that some families in her town couldn't afford to have a birthday party for their children. She felt everyone deserved to have a nice birthday, so she started making birthday boxes that included a cake mix, icing, balloons, and other items to celebrate a birthday. Bella collected donations from generous people in her community to help fill the boxes. And instead of getting presents for her own birthday, she asked for donations that could be given to others.

One of Bella's favorite memories was of delivering twenty packed birthday boxes to a women's shelter for moms and their kids who stayed there.

Bella's mom said: "Part of Bella's motivation to allow her story to be shared was a hope that other kids and adults would get involved in loving people in their own neighborhoods. She's a big believer in 'loving your neighbor,' no matter who or where they are. She hopes it will spark others to find a project they are interested in and jump in to help. Small things can make big differences."

Bella told *Good Morning America*, "I thank God for the opportunity, for letting me be able to shine my light and show that I love my neighbor."

"I THANK GOD FOR THE OPPORTUNITY, FOR LETTING ME BE ABLE TO SHINE MY LIGHT AND SHOW THAT I LOVE MY NEIGHBOR."

DONOVAN'S HEART: BIGGER THAN FOOTBALL

IN AUGUST OF 2018, EIGHT-YEAR-OLD DONOVAN Shaw was at a Seattle Seahawks football game with sixty other players from his youth football team. One boy from the group entered the stadium with the team, but he somehow got separated from his dad.

Donovan was busy watching pre-game warm-ups when he saw that this boy had tears in his eyes and looked scared to be in a huge stadium without his dad. Donovan went right over and invited the boy to sit next to him. He put his arm around him and made him feel welcome and safe until his father could get there. The boy immediately felt better. The two of them talked about football and the players on the field.

The boy who Donovan befriended that day still remembers the kindness that was shown to him. Donovan knows that acts of kindness don't have to be big to make a difference.

BIRTHDAY HUGS

I HAD BEEN SIX MONTHS SINCE EIGHTY-two-year-old Dan Peterson's wife had died. He really loved her and really missed her, and he had become sad and depressed. He was so lonely, now that his sweetheart was gone.

One day, Dan was in a grocery store, still sad and even *more* unhappy because he didn't like shopping. Out of nowhere, a four-year-old girl named Norah Wood saw Dan, jumped in front of him, and said, "Hi old person! It's my birthday today!" And with even more energy, Norah demanded a hug. Dan was surprised, but he allowed Norah to hug him anyway. He immediately began to feel happier and loved. Norah then asked her mom to take a picture of the two of them. It was the first time in nearly six months that Dan had started to feel a little joy. He got tears in his eyes and was very touched.

Norah's mom now takes Norah to visit Dan nearly every week.

"HI OLD PERSON! IT'S MY BIRTHDAY TODAY!"

"NO MATTER HOW TALL OR SMALL YOU ARE, WE *ALL* HAVE
THE ABILITY TO MAKE OUR WORLD A BETTER PLACE."

FROGS

By Julie Lourcey

I HAD SEEN THE MAN ON THE STREET CORNER MANY TIMES. MY SEVEN-YEAR OLD son, Will, had seen him, too, each time we exited the freeway going home from Will's baseball games. One day, Will asked me what the man's sign meant that read: *Need A Meal.* I explained there were people in our community who didn't have enough food to eat. Will didn't like this answer and felt bad that there were hungry people in the world. He decided to do something about it.

Will said, "Why drive by the man on the street corner and look the other way, when you can do something about it?" He decided to be a "doer." He started by raising awareness of the hungry and collecting food and donations for our local food bank. He loves to tell people, "Making a difference is easy if you follow these steps: See a need, make a plan, gather friends, and change the world!"

Will gathered his friends and formed a nonprofit called Friends Reaching Our Goals, or FROGs for short. The group's motto is "Having fun while helping others." So far, FROGs has helped provide over 900,000 meals for the hungry and engaged thousands of kids to make positive changes in the world.

Currently, Will and FROGs provide free catered meals of healthy food to kids through the FROGs Dinner Club. Once a month, they serve kids who are at risk of going hungry. After each healthy meal, these kids are then led in a service project.

Will says: "It's an epic feeling knowing I've inspired and empowered kids to know they have a voice and the ability to right a wrong in their community. No matter how tall or small you are, we *all* have the ability to make our world a better place."

FROM THE BOTTOM OF MY HEART

JAYDEN PEREZ'S MOM WAS GIVEN FREE TICKETS TO SEE A NEW YORK GIANTS FOOTBALL game, which happens to be Jayden's favorite team. He was so happy because of someone else's generosity to his family that he decided to find ways he could give to others to make them happy, too.

Well, Jayden is now ten and runs his own nonprofit called From the Bottom of My Heart. Here's a list of some of the things he has accomplished in just two years:

- Raised money to give to a girl from New York whose father had been shot and killed
- Donated food, supplies, and toiletries to people affected by the hurricane in Puerto Rico
- Held a toy drive for children in Puerto Rico, collecting over 1,100 toys for Christmas
- Used his own birthday money to buy food for abandoned pets in Puerto Rico
- Sent nearly $10,000 worth of clothes to Puerto Rico, which were donated to him by KidBox, a company where Jayden serves on their Kids' Board of Directors
- Collected and donated food, supplies, and pet food to people in Florida after the devastating Hurricane Michael
- Bought 160 flowers for Memorial Day to honor fallen soldiers, putting a flower on top of each grave and saluting each one in appreciation for their service
- Gave motivational speeches to groups on anti-bullying
- Bought and collected pajamas for kids in shelters
- Made Easter baskets for children who were in need
- Collected backpacks and school supplies to give to the less fortunate in his community

"Jayden hopes to inspire the younger generation to make a difference," his mom says. "He wants to continue changing the world with one act of kindness at a time."

And Jayden says, "Giving is the right thing to do. Giving is the best thing to do."

"GIVING IS THE RIGHT THING TO DO.
GIVING IS THE BEST THING TO DO."

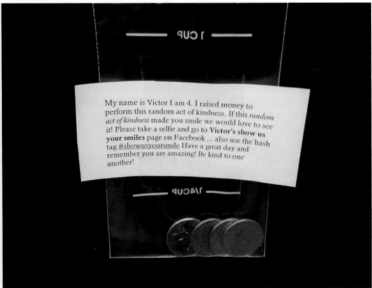

My name is Victor I am 4. I raised money to perform this random act of kindness. If this *random act of kindness* made you smile we would love to see it! Please take a selfie and go to **Victor's show us your smiles** page on Facebook ... also use the hash tag #showusyoursmile Have a great day and remember you are amazing! Be kind to one another!

Dear Victor,

You and your act of kindness at the barbershop yesterday impacted my life in such a wonderful way! The thing that may surprise you is how far reaching your thoughtful acts of kindness actually go because I was not even AT THE BARBERSHOP!! you gave a flower to my daughter Michalia. I was at home having a very sad day and Michalia texted me a photo of the flower and note attached to it (knowing my love for children and how much your story would mean to me and cheer me up). She was right! 👍😊 I am so proud of you and your giving spirit! You are a precious gift and you make this world a better place just by being YOU!! Thank you for reminding me that there are still loving, kind and thoughtful people in this world...a reminder that I really REALLY needed on the very same day that you were out in the world BEING that person!! This thank you note comes to you with the biggest hug that I have to give and a very big smile on my face! You are amazing, just a sweet little bright spot in the world!! XO from ██████████ ....your newest and biggest fan!!

WHEN HE HAS STEPPED OUT OF HIS COMFORT ZONE TO LOOK FOR OPPORTUNITIES TO SERVE OTHERS, HOWEVER, SOME OF THAT SHYNESS GOES AWAY.

RANDOM ACTS OF KINDNESS DAY

By Savannah Valencia

5 YEAR-OLD VICTOR VALENCIA IS TALKATIVE AROUND FAMILY AND FRIENDS, BUT he can be quite shy in public. When he has stepped out of his comfort zone to look for opportunities to serve others, however, some of that shyness goes away.

Victor loves first responders, such as police officers, firefighters, and paramedics. He loves the lights, the action, and the helping that is involved. After Victor visited their various stations, he decided he wanted to bring them goodies. He made a handful of law enforcement survival bags. The community heard what he was doing, and he received generous donations so he could make even more bags. In all, he delivered over one hundred bags to three different first responder stations!

Victor had so much fun doing the bags that he established a Random Acts of Kindness Day. On that day, he, his mom, and his sister do kind things for others like taking quarters and laundry soap to people at laundromats, bringing toys and treats for animals at the humane society, taking chocolates and flowers to volunteers, delivering snacks to six fire stations, bringing gift bags to the homeless veterans outreach program, and passing out dozens and dozens of flowers to random people.

Victor appreciates the importance of very small acts of kindness. For instance, he spent a day passing out coupons he had collected from kid's meals for a free custard to complete strangers. And one summer, when there was some construction going on in front of his house and the temperature reached record highs, Victor brought the workers frozen popsicles and gave them cold water and cookies. He had felt it was too hot for them.

BLESSING BAGS

LOGAN LYTLE IS SEVEN, AND HE LIKES TO WATCH ENTERTAINing YouTube videos. But one day, Logan saw videos of homeless people being helped by others and wanted to do something like that himself. That's when he came up with the idea of Blessing Bags—bags filled with a few essential items such as bottles of water, wet wipes, lotion, snacks, and even gift cards.

According to his dad, Larry, Logan has always liked to help others, so it was not unusual that Logan wanted to assemble the bags. Inside each bag, he put a note, and the note said:

> *I am praying for you! Here is a blessing bag for you to carry through the day. Please know that I am praying for you right now. Know that nothing is impossible if you keep your faith and trust in God.*
>
> *Love,*
> *Logan*
>
> *"Do not worry about tomorrow, tomorrow will take care of itself. Each day has enough trouble of its own." —Matthew 6:34*

So far, Logan has given blessing bags to over twenty people! He says, "I feel bad for homeless people, and it makes me proud to be able to help them."

"IT MAKES ME PROUD TO BE ABLE TO HELP THEM."

BUT THEN I WATCHED HIM
APPROACH A YOUNGER
GIRL, TEAR HIS PIECE OF
THE SANDWICH IN TWO,
AND HAND HALF TO HER.

SHARING HALF IS SHARING ALL

By Gabriel Morris

IN MARCH OF 2015, I WENT ON A HUMANITARIAN TRIP TO THE COUNTRY OF Ghana in Africa. The people have so little, yet they find ways to give so much. Our group was visiting a school in a village called Akrapong. After a long day, teachers showed us around the village and introduced us to some of the students' families. I noticed how simple their living conditions were.

The parents explained their daily routines and what chores their children did every day. The children would wake up early to help clean and prepare food and work in their small gardens or farms. Then they would eat a small breakfast and get ready for school. At school, they were provided one meal, and their next meal would probably be breakfast the next morning. After school, the children would walk home and work on afternoon chores. Somehow, they found time to finish their homework. I was amazed they could make it all work.

As we sat down to eat lunch that day, I remember pulling out of my backpack a peanut butter and jelly sandwich and feeling fortunate for having even one sandwich. To my side was a boy who was about six years old, staring right at me. I gestured for him to come over. I tore my sandwich in two and gave him half. I expected him to eat it right away, but he just stared at it for a little while, then walked away. I was confused. But then I watched him approach a younger girl, tear his piece of the sandwich in two, and hand half to her. As they ate their small pieces of sandwich, I thought, "These wonderful people, who have so little, really have it all. They know how to share everything they have with each other."

BIG SISTERS AND LITTLE BROTHERS

I **AM THE SECOND OLDEST OF SIX CHILDREN IN MY FAMILY.** As the only girl, I have always felt I should be a good example to my brothers. Never did I think my brothers would be an example of kindness to me, but each one really has helped me.

One of my younger brothers, Will, who is now thirteen, has served me lovingly and unconditionally most of my life. Most of the time it has been through small acts of kindness, but I can remember each one.

I really like to eat snacks. In fact, if someone's treats go missing, I am usually the first one they look at. If I ask Will if I could have some of his treats, he would always share at least half with me—or sometimes the whole thing. He would say, "Hmm, I really like this, but since I love you, you can have it!"

At one point in my life, Will was aware that I was struggling with low self-esteem. One time we were shopping together, and I had a little meltdown in public. Will saw I was having a difficult time. He put his arms around me, gave me a big hug, and said, "Sammie, you are the prettiest person I know!"

Will doesn't serve only me. I hear stories about Will being especially kind to kids who don't have a lot of friends. He's humble, kind, and compassionate, and I'm sure he will continue to have an impact on many people just by being kind.

"SAMMIE, YOU ARE
THE PRETTIEST
PERSON I KNOW!"

A FORCE FOR GOOD

FOUR-YEAR-OLD CHASE HANSEN AND HIS DAD, JOHN, HAD just attended the FanX Salt Lake Comic Convention where they learned about superheroes. Chase loves superheroes, and he wanted to be a superhero and do good in the world. So, he and his dad started a project called Kid Labs with the mission to be a force for good.

They called their first project Project Empathy and worked together to help people who were homeless. They would sit down and eat a meal with people who were living on the streets and find out more about them. By the time Chase was nine, he and his dad had met with and helped more than 130 homeless people.

One time, they helped pick up the children of a father who was struggling. They also gave the father a bike so he would have transportation. Other times, they have just listened while others talked. Sometimes Chase is asked what he does to help people who are homeless, and he replies, "Just be their friends!" Chase's dad says, "From what I see on the news, the world could use a hero. Besides, the greatest stories are the ones you can be a part of."

Perhaps their best superhero story is when Chase's dad—and Kid Labs—were going through some hard times themselves. Chase kept his positive attitude and his desire to be a force for good in the world, but this time, he was a superhero for his dad. John said, "Chase believed in me until I could believe in myself again. His frequent 'I love you, Dad!' kept me anchored. It was the medicine for my soul I needed to reboot and find a purpose."

"FROM WHAT I SEE ON THE NEWS, THE WORLD COULD USE A HERO. BESIDES, THE GREATEST STORIES ARE THE ONES YOU CAN BE A PART OF."

DONATING HAIR— WITH HEART

T HE THREE JAMES SISTERS, WHO ARE FROM Australia, had been growing their hair since they were born. Abbie is five, Charlee is eight, and Bella is eleven. On their Everyday Hero donation page, they said, "We have made the decision to make a difference by cutting and donating our hair to be made into three wigs for some special people who have lost their hair due to a medical condition."

Hair loss is one of the more visible results of being treated for cancer, so many patients want to get a wig. But a nice wig can cost over $6,000, so by donating their own hair, the James sisters will help three families save a lot of money! They were also able to increase awareness for children with cancer and raise over $2,500 in donations.

"WE HAVE MADE THE DECISION TO MAKE A DIFFERENCE BY CUTTING AND DONATING OUR HAIR TO BE MADE INTO THREE WIGS FOR SOME SPECIAL PEOPLE WHO HAVE LOST THEIR HAIR DUE TO A MEDICAL CONDITION."

IT WAS A HOT DAY,
AND JENNY, WHO WAS
EIGHT, SAW HOW HARD
THEY WERE WORKING
AND WANTED TO
DO SOMETHING TO
ACKNOWLEDGE THEIR
SERVICE.

AMBULANCE SNACKS

JENNY THOMAS AND HER MOM HAD SEEN A FEW ambulances pass them earlier in the day. It was a hot day, and Jenny, who was eight, saw how hard they were working and wanted to do something to acknowledge their service.

Jenny lives in Carmarthen, Wales, where emergency medical employees from Welsh Ambulance Service had just transferred a patient to the hospital. While the ambulance workers were still inside the hospital, Jenny asked her mom if they could buy water and snacks for them. She placed the water bottles and snacks on their ambulance. When the ambulance workers saw Jenny's gifts, they were very grateful for her thoughtfulness. It was a simple act, but it meant a lot to the workers to know that their service was appreciated.

THE "PATIENT" RETURNS

C LAIRE NOLAND HAD CANCER AND HAD to receive treatments for over six months at Lucile Packard Children's Hospital at Stanford in Palo Alto, California. Claire was six years old at the time. In July of 2018, on the last day of her chemotherapy treatment, her parents told her that they would take her anywhere she wanted to go to celebrate being cancer free—the beach, the park, shopping, anywhere!

But Claire said no to all of those places. Instead, she wanted to go back to the hospital to spread love and hope to patients who were still there. So, the next day, they returned to the same hospital and the same floor—not as a patient, but as a friend to cheer on those she had come to know. She had made signs with encouraging messages to leave with them.

Claire's mom, Lindsey, said: "One of the most valuable gifts Claire gave was her time. Knowing there were children still fighting for healing compelled her to do everything in her power to bring them joy. I could think of no better way to spend our first day of being cancer free!"

"IT'S JUST REALLY COOL THAT I'M GETTING MORE PEOPLE TO HONOR VETERANS. I'LL DO ANYTHING TO MAKE A VETERAN HAPPY!"

FLAGS AND FLOWERS FOR VETERANS

PRESTON SHARP'S GRANDPA SERVED HIS COUNTRY IN THE US NAVY. PEOPLE who serve in the military, such as in the navy, army, air force, or marine corps, serve and sometimes sacrifice their lives for the safety of citizens of the United States. We can think of them as heroes.

You might say Preston Sharp is a kind of hero. He's twelve, but his grandpa died before he ever had the chance to meet him. Three years ago, he and his mom went to visit his grandpa's grave. Preston expected to see flags and flowers on the graves of veterans to honor them, but he and his mom were disappointed when they didn't see any. This inspired him with an idea.

That night, Preston told his mom that he wanted to start putting flags and flowers on every single veteran's grave. His mom, April, asked him how they were going to be able to afford it, and he said, "I'm going to start a GoFundMe." It took some time and some hard work, but they raised enough money to pay for flags and flowers to put on over 4,000 veteran's graves.

Two-and-a-half years later, Preston has decorated over 220,000 veteran's graves in thirty different states! He now has a nonprofit called Veterans Flags and Flowers. And he hasn't stopped there. He is still working to raise money and challenges others to place a flag and a flower on a veteran's grave. Preston said, "It's just really cool that I'm getting more people to honor veterans. I'll do anything to make a veteran happy!"

BUCKETS OF CARDS FOR A BUDDY

ANDEN WILFONG AND OLIVER PLEUNE ARE BUDDIES AND FIRST MET WHEN they were about three years old. Each has an older brother who played basketball, so they became good friends while watching from the sidelines of those games.

Oliver is fighting a rare disease called cystic fibrosis that damages his lungs and digestive system. He has to take medications every day and go through a lot of special breathing treatments to keep his lungs working properly. Every year, about 1,000 more people find out they have this disease.

Oliver was recently in the hospital being treated for a lung infection, and Landen came each day to visit him. Landen didn't like his buddy having to stay in the hospital and wanted to do something to cheer him up. So, he decided to ask his school classmates to make get-well cards. When the cards were delivered to Oliver, Oliver was so excited that Landen decided to encourage his entire school to make even more cards! Each day Oliver was in the hospital, Landen brought him buckets full of cards, but what he was really delivering was happiness and hope.

It has always been hard for Landen to see his friend struggle with this disease, so when Landen was invited to participate in a charity event called Fashion Breathes Life, he was excited and jumped right in. This event raises money for the Cystic Fibrosis Foundation, who is helping find a cure to heal people like Oliver. Landen wants to help them achieve that goal, but to be part of the event, he had to raise $2,000. But instead, he set a goal of raising $10,000! And with the help of many generous people, he was able to raise over $42,000 for the Cystic Fibrosis Foundation!

Oliver's mom, Jill, says, "Landen is always thinking of others. He shows so much compassion and kindness. He's an example to all of us of what it means to be a true friend." He will keep on helping his buddy and others who have cystic fibrosis.

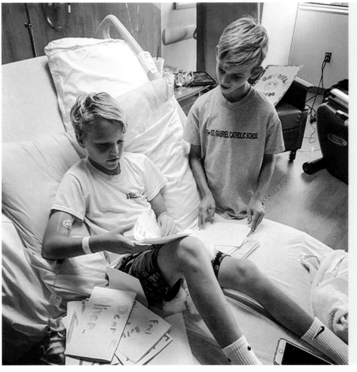

"HE'S AN EXAMPLE TO ALL OF US OF WHAT IT
MEANS TO BE A TRUE FRIEND."

RHETT'S LEGACY OF KINDNESS

By Lorna Hering

SCRIPTURE SAYS THAT GOD GIVES GOOD GIFTS TO ALL OF his children. Those gifts may be talent-based, looks-based, personality-based, action-based, or heart-based, and they are, indeed, all good. Occasionally, I believe God gives someone such an amazing gift that it defines their life, becomes their purpose, and blesses everyone who comes into contact with that gift.

Rhett Hering was blessed with such a gift. From the very beginning, Rhett was filled with love, kindness, joy, and a unique ability to find the good in all people and to not see barriers. His blonde hair, dimples, blue eyes, and contagious smile could light up any room. Being kind to people, spreading joy, and making people feel valued were attributes that were ingrained in his soul; it was just who he was. There was no "work" involved for him to do kind things or validate people. It was just how he was created.

Often you would find Rhett at church or even the grocery store, helping or hugging an elderly man or woman and loving on them in ways that were almost supernatural. He was quick to befriend new kids at school and make them feel welcome. Rhett often commented on people's smiles. He loved to hear people laugh and see people happy. He freely gave of his time and invested his heart in loving those around him in big and small ways. He never did these things to be noticed; he just genuinely loved to make other people feel special. He loved younger kids and always found ways to include them in activities instead of treating them like they were a bother. Rhett never struggled to overlook economic issues, racial issues, or ugly labels that people often place on others, because he simply did not see those things. He saw people as treasures to be embraced and loved.

One time, we had a coach thank us for allowing Rhett to give some new shoes to a kid in his PE class that didn't have workout shoes. We didn't know what the coach was talking about. When we asked Rhett, he just said that he had given away one of his best pairs of shoes to a nice kid in his class who needed them. He had no intention of telling us because he had not done it for show or for recognition. He had just seen a need and had found a way to help.

Maybe my favorite story involving Rhett's kindness happened one Christmas morning. Our family was driving home from an early morning stocking and gift exchange at Rhett's grandparents' house. Rhett's stocking had contained a large bag of beef jerky, which was Rhett's absolute favorite. As we approached an intersection, Rhett noticed a homeless man holding a sign. From the back seat, Rhett said, "Wait, Dad. Stop, stop, stop. This man needs a Christmas gift."

Rhett started frantically looking through his toys and stocking stuffers to find something he could give a grown man. All of a sudden, he eyed the unopened bag of beef jerky. With a huge smile, he threw it to his dad in the front seat and told him to give it to the man. When his dad handed the man the bag of beef jerky, the man smiled, pumped his arms in the air, and said, "Thank you! Beef jerky is my favorite!"

Rhett smiled back at the man and yelled out the window, "Mine too! Merry Christmas!"

That simple act of kindness and the happiness shown by that man left such an impact on our whole family that we began making bags to hand out to homeless people—and all the bags contained beef jerky.

On December 28, 2015, Rhett's life was tragically cut short by an ATV accident in front of our house. Our hearts were absolutely shattered. At the funeral, the preacher said that a love like Rhett's could start a revolution. In the weeks and years since losing our son, we have heard countless stories of Rhett's big heart and kindness. He blessed so many people in so many unique and kind ways while he was alive, and some amazing acts of kindness have been done in his honor since he passed away. The Rhett Revolution was founded shortly after his death. It is a nonprofit organization designed to serve, help, and bless people. Our mission is to spread kindness through activities such as running a food pantry, educating kids on the importance of kindness, serving bereaved parents, and encouraging college students.

Although Rhett was only on earth for a short fifteen years, he truly did leave a legacy of kindness.

A LOVE LIKE RHETT'S COULD
START A REVOLUTION.

MY IDEAS AND PLANS

(Use this space to write down ideas that come to your mind as you read the stories.)

(Use this space to write down your plan on what you will do to help make the world a better place.)

_____   _____

_____   _____

_____   _____

_____   _____

_____   _____

_____   _____

_____   _____

_____   _____

_____   _____

_____   _____

_____   _____

PHOTO CREDITS

- Help Me Color a Rainbow: Photo by Gary Michael's Photography

- He Stopped to Help Someone In Need: Photo by Riley Duncan

- Life Savings—Saving Lives: Photo by Jeffrey Becker, Photographer, *USA Today* Sports Images

- Liam's Lunches of Love: Photo courtesy of GoFundMe Kid Heroes: GoFundMe.com/liamslunchesoflove

- My Life Will Be About Giving: Photos by Rebecca Stumpf

- Donovan's Heart: Bigger than Football: Photo by Chelsea Burke

- Additional photos licensed from Shutterstock.com artists: Lopolo (page 2), ANURAK PONGPATIMET (page 7), Rawpixel.com (page 8), bbernard (page 10), Evgeny Atamanenko (pages 12-13)